P9-CDM-749

Tolerance

BY CYNTHIA AMOROSO

Published by The Child's World®
1980 Lookout Drive • Mankato, MN 56003-1705
800-599-READ • www.childsworld.com

Acknowledgments
The Child's World®: Mary Berendes, Publishing Director
The Design Lab: Design
Pamela J. Mitsakos: Photo Research
Christine Florie: Editing

Photographs ©: David M. Budd Photography: 11, 15, 21; iStockphoto.
com/archives: 13; iStockphoto.com/BlueOrange Studio: 19; iStockphoto.
com/CEFutcher: cover, 1; iStockphoto.com/ChristopherBernard: 9;
iStockphoto.com/Kali Nine LLC: 17; iStockphoto.com/Steve Debenport
Imagery: 7; iStockphoto.com/bonniej graphic design: 5.

ISBN 9781623235277
LCCN 2013931456

Printed in the United States of America
Mankato, MN
July, 2013
PA02172

ABOUT THE AUTHOR

Cynthia Amoroso is Director of Curriculum and Instruction for a school district in Minnesota. She enjoys reading, writing, gardening, traveling, and spending time with friends and family.

Table of Contents

What Is Tolerance?

People come in all shapes, sizes, and colors. They have different ways of life. They speak all kinds of languages. They wear their hair in different ways. They eat different kinds of foods. They listen to all kinds of music. Tolerance is **accepting** differences in other people. It is thinking, "It is OK that you are different from me!"

Learning from our differences can be fun!

Tolerance at School

Maybe your class is having a **discussion**. The teacher asks all of you to share your ideas. One student has an idea that is different from yours. You show tolerance by listening to the idea. You understand that more than one idea can be **worthwhile**.

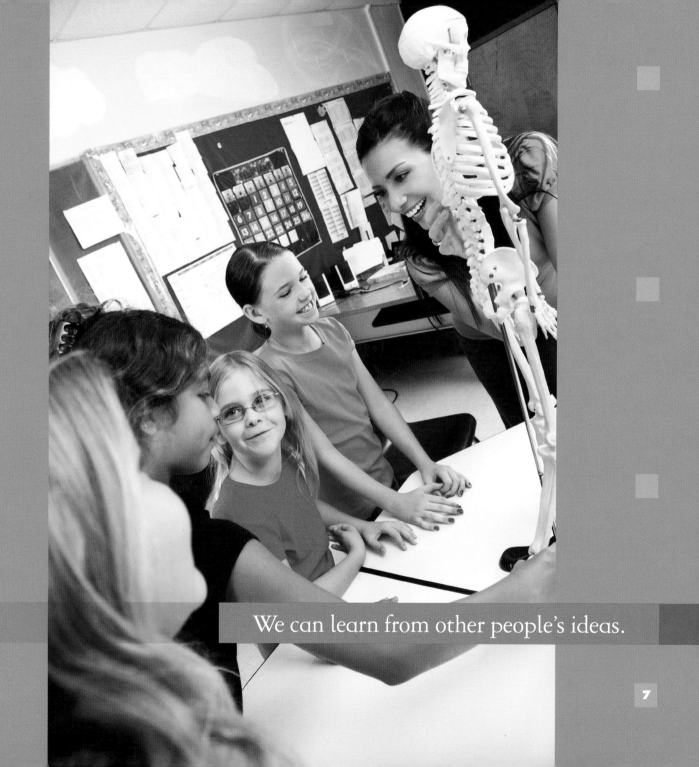

We can learn from other people's ideas.

Tolerance and Your Friends

One of your friends does not speak English well. Everybody around her is talking fast. She does not understand what they are saying. You show tolerance by helping her understand. You explain what they are saying. You do not make fun of her for needing your help.

Differences can make our lives more interesting.

Tolerance on the Playground

Some kids in your class might not have many friends. They might act differently from other kids. On the playground, nobody asks them to play. You can see that they feel left out. You show tolerance by asking them to play. You and your friends make them feel welcome.

Tolerance at Home

You and your brother like to watch TV. You like to watch cartoons. Your brother likes nature shows. You show tolerance by letting your brother watch his show. The next day, he shows tolerance by letting you watch cartoons!

Tolerance means accepting that people like different things.

Tolerance in Your Neighborhood

You and your family go to a church in town. You have beliefs about many things. Your neighbors do not go to your church. They have different beliefs from yours. You show tolerance for their ideas. You accept that they believe different things.

Tolerance means respecting other people's beliefs.

15

Tolerance and Newcomers

You have lived in your neighborhood for a long time. One day a new family moves in. They speak and dress differently. They cook different foods. You show tolerance by making them feel welcome. You try to learn about how they do things.

Maybe your new neighbors will become your new friends!

Tolerance toward Younger Kids

Maybe you have a little sister. She always wants to tag along. She wants to go everywhere you go. She wants to do everything you do. But she is too little to do some things. She does not know as much as you, either. Sometimes she seems like a pest! But you show tolerance by being nice to her. You understand that she is just young.

Being tolerant toward your sister is more fun than being mad!

Tolerance Helps Us All Get Along

Showing tolerance makes the world around us much friendlier. If we are tolerant, we can be OK with our differences. We can try to understand one another. We can learn from each other. We can work together. And we can have fun together!

Tolerance makes life more fun!

Glossary

accept–When you accept something, you are OK with it.

discussion–When people have a discussion, they talk about something.

worthwhile–If something is worthwhile, it is useful.

Learn More

Books

Copsey, Susan Elizabeth, and Barnabas Kindersley. *Children Just Like Me*. New York: Dorling Kindersley, 1995.

Fox, Mem. *Whoever You Are*. Orlando, FL: Voyager Books, 2006.

Yunger, Joshua. *Hippo and Monkey*. Piermont, NH: Bunker Hill Publishing, 2012.

Web Sites

Visit our Web site for links about tolerance: childsworld.com/links

Note to Parents, Teachers, and Librarians: We routinely verify our Web links to make sure they are safe and active sites. So encourage your readers to check them out!

Index